Co-occurring Disorders Series

PREVENTING RELAPSE
Revised

Dennis C. Daley, Ph.D.

FORMERLY THE DUAL DIAGNOSIS SERIES

Hazelden
Center City, Minnesota 55012-0176

1-800-328-9000
1-651-213-4590 (Fax)
www.hazelden.org

©1993, 2003 by Hazelden Foundation
All rights reserved. First edition 1993
Second edition 2003
Printed in the United States of America

This published work is protected by the law of copyright. Duplicating all or part of this work by any means without obtaining permission from the publisher is an illegal act. Unauthorized copying of this material violates the rights of the publisher and is directly contrary to the principles of honesty, respect, and dignity toward others, which is the foundation of Hazelden's and many of its customers' reputations and success.

To request permission, write to
Permissions Coordinator, Hazelden, P.O. Box 176, Center City, MN 55012-0176.
To purchase additional copies of this publication, call
1-800-328-9000 or 1-651-213-4000.

ISBN: 1-59285-006-5

Editor's note
This material was written to educate individuals about chemical dependency and mental illness. It is not intended as a substitute for professional medical or psychiatric care.

Any stories or case studies that may be used in this material are composites of many individuals. Names and details have been changed to protect identities.

Cover design by Lightbourne
Interior design by Lightbourne

CONTENTS

1. Introduction to Relapse Prevention
   and Co-occurring Disorders 1

2. Causes of Relapse 5

3. Recovery Tools Checklist 11

4. Managing Relapse Warning Signs 15

5. Daily Symptom and Problem Checklist 21

6. Managing Feelings to Reduce Relapse Risk 25

7. Coping with Negative Thoughts
   to Reduce Relapse Risk 31

8. Developing and Using a Relapse
   Prevention Support System 37

9. Coping with Emergencies 41

10. Summary of Strategies for Recovery
    and Relapse Prevention 45

11. Final Thoughts 49

ONE

INTRODUCTION TO RELAPSE PREVENTION AND CO-OCCURRING DISORDERS

People with co-occurring, or dual, disorders have chemical dependency (also called addiction or substance abuse) and a psychiatric illness (also called a mental illness). If you are in recovery, it is possible to relapse to chemical dependency and to your psychiatric illness. Understanding relapse and developing a relapse prevention plan is an important part of recovery from co-occurring disorders. A relapse prevention plan outlines the steps you will take to help yourself when problems arise that could lead to a relapse to your psychiatric symptoms or your addiction.

> Understanding relapse and developing a relapse prevention plan is an important part of recovery from co-occurring disorders.

This workbook was written to help you develop your relapse prevention plan. Review your completed workbook tasks with your therapist or counselor, doctor, or sponsor. Also share this workbook with family members or significant others who care about you and support your recovery. Because "poor judgment" is a symptom of some psychiatric disorders, it is especially important to involve others who can assist you when you do not realize you need help. This process of sharing your plan with others and asking for their input helps you work a "we" program instead of an "I" program.

You do not have to complete every section of this workbook. Choose the ones that seem most important to you at this time. Also, do not rush through the reading and the activities. Take time to "try out" a new recovery idea before you move on to the next one.

This workbook covers the following topics:

- definitions and causes of relapse
- using a recovery checklist
- relapse warning signs
- using a daily checklist
- managing upsetting or negative feelings
- managing negative thoughts
- using a relapse prevention support system
- coping with emergencies
- summary of strategies for recovery and relapse prevention

Definitions of Relapse

With addiction, relapse is the process of returning to alcohol or other drug use. You can be in relapse even before you start using alcohol or other drugs again. This is called a *relapse process,* or *building up to use.*

With psychiatric illness, relapse means that the symptoms of your illness return after a period of improvement. For some people, this means that their symptoms come back after being absent for a while. For others, it means that their symptoms get a lot worse.

> With psychiatric illness, relapse means that the symptoms of your illness return after a period of improvement.

Relapse prevention is your plan of action that will help you cope with your co-occurring disorders on an ongoing basis. Prevention involves learning about the causes and signs of relapse and developing ways to deal with them. It also involves using a support system, receiving professional treatment, and attending self-help group meetings, such as Alcoholics Anonymous (AA), Narcotics Anonymous (NA), Cocaine Anonymous (CA), Mentally Ill Substance Abuser (MISA), Dual Recovery Anonymous (DRA), or other recovery programs.

Effects of Relapse

The effects of a relapse to a mental disorder or addiction depend on the severity of the relapse and whether you take action quickly to get the help you need to stop it. Effects may vary from mild to serious. It is not possible to know ahead of time what the effects will be or how serious they will be. This is why a relapse prevention plan is so important.

> The effects of a relapse to a mental disorder or addiction depend on the severity of the relapse.

Some examples of relapses from men and women in recovery follow. Notice the differences in how long they were sober or stable from psychiatric symptoms before they relapsed. Also notice the different outcomes of their relapses.

> I started drinking after ten years of sobriety. At first, it was just a few beers. Then, it escalated and got out of control. I quit taking lithium and seeing my doctor and therapist. My family had to commit me. I ended up separating from my wife of twenty-four years and almost lost my business. It took a long time to put my life back together.
>
> *David, age 48*

After over one year of feeling good, my depression came back. This took me by surprise because my life had improved so much. I became suicidal and despondent, but with the encouragement of my friends in NA, I got help from my doctor and therapist. I'm back on track now. Thank God I didn't use cocaine, although the thought crossed my mind.

Marissa, age 36

An old party friend stopped over to my apartment. On impulse, I smoked pot with him even though I had been drug free for over nine months. He sold me some pot, and I smoked all weekend. I became psychotic and busted up my apartment, causing a lot of damage, which I'm still paying for. My landlord kicked me out, and I was homeless for a while—all because of smoking some damn pot and not following my plan.

James, age 33

I had an argument with a man I was dating. So I bought a bottle, took a few drinks, and called him. Before hanging up on him, I threatened to go to his house and make a big scene. I even thought about cutting myself in front of him. Instead, I called my sponsor who helped me calm myself down and stop things before they got out of hand.

Elaine, age 25

TWO

CAUSES OF RELAPSE

Many factors lead to relapse to one or both of your disorders. A return of your psychiatric symptoms can make you feel like using alcohol or other drugs again. And using alcohol or other drugs can trigger psychiatric symptoms or interfere with your recovery from a mental disorder. Alcohol and street drugs can change the effects of psychiatric medications and lower your motivation to attend treatment sessions or support group meetings.

Relapse is usually caused by several factors working together. Here are some of the more common causes of relapse to co-occurring disorders:

> **Relapse is usually caused by several factors working together.**

Failing to Follow Your Treatment Plan

- missing appointments with your doctor, therapist, or counselor
- missing sessions in your partial-hospitalization or intensive outpatient program
- cutting down on or not attending support group meetings
- stopping therapy or counseling without talking it over with your therapist first
- stopping your medication or not taking it as prescribed
- not making the changes you agreed to as part of your treatment plan

Ignoring Your Early Relapse Warning Signs

- not taking action when your symptoms return or worsen
- not taking action when you show behavior that puts your recovery in jeopardy

Emotional Distress

- feeling very upset or angry
- feeling depressed
- feeling isolated or alone
- feeling empty or useless
- feeling overwhelmed or stressed out

Lifestyle Factors

- having no structure or routine in your life
- having no goals or direction in your life
- experiencing major life changes or negative events, such as the severe illness or death of a family member, the loss of a job, or a major money problem

Relationship Difficulties

- experiencing serious conflict with another person
- feeling unloved or emotionally distant from others
- having trouble communicating with important people in your life
- feeling stuck in bad relationships that cause too much pain

Spending Time with Abusers of Alcohol or Other Drugs

- hanging out with other substance abusers who get high

- staying involved with a partner who gets high

Spending Time with People Who Do Not Support Your Efforts to Change

- staying involved with people who are negative or hostile toward you
- staying involved with people who do not support your efforts to change
- hanging out with people who try to persuade you to stop treatment
- hanging out with people who try to get you to stop attending support group meetings

Thinking You Are Cured (the Return of Denial)

- thinking that since you have been clean and sober for a while, you are no longer addicted
- thinking that since your chronic depression has lifted, you no longer need treatment
- thinking that since you have not had serious symptoms of your disorder in a while, you no longer have an illness, or you no longer need treatment or medication

Lack of Coping Skills to Solve Problems

- lack of skills in developing and keeping relationships
- difficulty dealing with negative feelings or emotions (e.g., anger, depression)
- difficulty dealing with negative thoughts
- difficulty coping with normal life issues such as going on job interviews, budgeting money, or getting the resources or services you need

Personality Factors

- being too stubborn to listen to the advice of your treatment team, sponsor, or other members of support groups
- acting before thinking of the consequences of your behavior (being impulsive)
- wanting others to solve your problems
- avoiding facing your problems or conflicts head-on

Other Factors

- going back to work or taking on responsibilities too soon after an episode of illness that required hospitalization
- taking a medication for one illness that triggers symptoms of another illness
- getting the wrong type of treatment for your illnesses

Also, some people are more sensitive to stress and normal life experiences as a result of their biological and psychological makeup. Others are more seriously affected by their psychiatric illness or addiction. As a result, these people are more vulnerable to relapse.

Recovery Activity

Describe one relapse risk factor that could lead you back to using alcohol or other drugs.

_____

_____

Coping strategies I can use to manage this relapse risk factor:

_____
_____
_____
_____
_____

Kathy's Plan

"When pressure builds up and things really get to me, I wonder, *Why even bother with recovery? A few drinks would make me feel good.* Then I start telling myself that I'm really not an alcoholic because I've been sober for a while. To cope with this risk factor for relapse, I take four steps: (1) I remind myself that my history has proven me dead wrong; I have never been able to control my drinking, and I can't become a nonalcoholic. (2) I review the benefits of staying clean, because the truth is, no matter how bad things get, staying sober really is worth it. (3) I talk about what's bothering me with my sponsor and AA group to get support. (4) I go to the gym to work out, because a brisk physical workout always helps me release built-up tension."

Recovery Activity

Describe one relapse risk factor that could cause your psychiatric symptoms to return or worsen.

_____
_____

Duplicating this page is illegal. Do not copy this material without written permission from the publisher.

Coping strategies I can use to manage this relapse risk factor:

_____
_____
_____
_____
_____

Jack's Plan

"When my depression has lifted for a couple weeks, I sometimes tell myself that I'm cured and don't need medicine or treatment any longer. Stopping treatment is a big relapse risk factor for me. Whenever I have any thoughts of stopping treatment, I take the following steps: (1) I remind myself that I have recurrent depression, which is best treated by staying on medication and staying in therapy, even when my symptoms have improved. (2) I remind myself of the many improvements I experience when I stay in treatment. (3) I tell my doctor or therapist that I've been thinking about not taking my medication. (4) I tell my wife I'm thinking about not taking my medication."

THREE

RECOVERY TOOLS CHECKLIST

Recovery is an active process in which you work on managing your disorders and improving the quality of your life. Recovery involves making changes in yourself and your lifestyle. While you do many things on your own to recover, getting help and support from others is vital. Professionals; friends in AA, NA, CA, DRA, or mental health support groups; family members; or others important in your life can provide support to you. You need not recover alone.

You improve your chances of staying well and staying off alcohol and other drugs if you use your "tools of recovery." These tools are the steps you take to help yourself get better and deal with problems head-on when they occur. Use some of your recovery tools every day, because they can serve as "protection" against relapse.

> You improve your chances of staying well and staying off alcohol and other drugs if you use your "tools of recovery."

Recovery Activity

For each day of the week, place a check next to the recovery tools that you used.

RECOVERY TOOLS	M	T	W	Th	F	S	S
I attended AA, NA, or CA.							
I went to a DRA or mental health support group meeting.							
I talked with my sponsor.							
I talked with a supportive person.							
I talked with a member of my relapse prevention support network.							
I attended a session with my doctor, counselor, or therapy group.							
I took my medication for my mental health disorder only as prescribed.							
I meditated, prayed, or used my Higher Power.							
I got physical exercise.							
I read recovery literature.							
I wrote in a recovery journal or workbook.							
I participated in a pleasant activity.							
I fought off urges to use substances.							
I practiced positive thinking and fought off negative thoughts.							
I used emotional coping skills to manage my feelings.							
I reviewed my day to identify relapse warning signs or high-risk situations.							
I devised a plan to manage relapse risk factors or warning signs.							
I followed my daily plan for recovery.							

Duplicating this page is illegal. Do not copy this material without written permission from the publisher.

Other recovery tools that I used this week or steps I took to help myself:

_____
_____
_____
_____
_____
_____

Describe the benefits you experienced as a result of using your recovery tools.

_____
_____
_____
_____
_____
_____

Because I did not use enough recovery tools this past week, I experienced the following difficulties:

_____
_____
_____
_____
_____
_____

FOUR

MANAGING RELAPSE WARNING SIGNS

Usually, before a full-blown episode of relapse to psychiatric illness or addiction occurs, changes show up that indicate your symptoms are getting worse. Sometimes these changes happen pretty quickly. Other times they happen gradually, over a period of weeks or longer.

These changes are *relapse warning signs*. They show in your attitudes, thoughts, moods, behaviors, health habits, and daily routine. By catching your relapse warning signs early, it is possible to head off a relapse before it starts or to stop it early.

> By catching your relapse warning signs early, it is possible to head off a relapse before it starts or to stop it early.

Recovery Activity

The following are examples of relapse warning signs that are common to different psychiatric illnesses as well as to addiction. Remember, even though there are many common signs, everyone has a unique set of relapse warning signs. By identifying your warning signs, you put yourself in a position to make your recovery go better. Review the list. Do any of the signs apply to you?

If you have relapsed before, think about the days or weeks before your symptoms returned. As you read the following lists of warning signs, try to recall if any of them were present. Place a check next to each warning sign that you believe was present before you relapsed to your psychiatric illness or to alcohol or other drug use.

Changes in Attitudes and Thoughts

__ I quit caring about my recovery program.
__ I thought I could handle my problems on my own without treatment.
__ I thought I no longer needed to take medication or go to treatment sessions.
__ I quit caring about myself or what happened to me.
__ I had negative and hopeless thoughts about the future.
__ I became critical of my doctor, therapist, sponsor, case manager, or people in my support group.
__ My thoughts raced, became confused, or did not make any sense.
__ My thoughts became paranoid. I thought that people were out to get me, that they were laughing at me, or that they were talking about me.
__ I started hallucinating (hearing voices that did not exist).
__ I thought life was not worth living and thought of ending it all.
__ I thought drinking alcohol or using other drugs would help me feel better and improve my condition.
__ When thinking about the future, I always expected the worst.
__ I thought I could control my use of alcohol or other drugs.
__ I thought I would be okay if I stayed away from my main drug of abuse and used something else (e.g., I didn't do crack but still smoked pot or drank alcohol).
__ I thought about hurting someone else.
__ I thought about ways to scam others or break the law.

Changes in Mood

__ My moods shifted rapidly from feeling up to feeling depressed.
__ I became more and more sad or depressed.
__ I felt increasingly anxious, nervous, agitated, or edgy.
__ My mood became manic, and I felt on top of the world.

Duplicating this page is illegal. Do not copy this material without written permission from the publisher.

__ I felt very fearful and overwhelmed by feelings of panic.
__ I felt very resentful, angry, or hostile.
__ I felt empty, like nothing was important in life.
__ I felt guilty or shameful.
__ I felt lonely and isolated.
__ I felt very excited and very good about things.
__ I felt like I needed some "action."
__ I felt unable to enjoy anything in life.

Changes in Behavior

__ I canceled or failed to show for treatment sessions with my doctor or therapist.
__ I stopped going to treatment sessions completely.
__ I quit taking my medications or did not take them as prescribed.
__ I cut down on or stopped attending my AA, NA, CA, DRA, or mental health support group meetings.
__ I called my sponsor or other support people less often or stopped calling altogether.
__ I stopped taking care of my responsibilities (at home or at work).
__ I withdrew from or ignored other people, preferring to keep to myself.
__ I argued or fought with others.
__ I hurt myself or hurt someone else.
__ I quit using my recovery tools. (See page 12.)
__ I began to talk slower, faster, or in ways that confused others.
__ I acted in ways that were unlike me, ways that others thought were bizarre or strange.
__ I socialized with other people less or stopped socializing altogether.
__ I quit doing activities that were fun, such as hobbies I enjoyed.
__ I started doing things that were against the law.

Changes in Health Habits or Daily Routines

__ I quit following my recovery plan and did not do the things I needed to do to feel better and stay straight.

Duplicating this page is illegal. Do not copy this material without written permission from the publisher.

__ I began sleeping much more than usual.
__ I began sleeping much less than usual.
__ I had problems falling asleep, staying asleep, or waking up earlier than I planned.
__ My energy level increased quite a bit.
__ My energy level decreased quite a bit.
__ My appetite increased greatly.
__ My appetite decreased greatly.
__ I quit exercising.
__ My daily routines changed a great deal.

Other Addictions or Compulsive Behaviors

__ I spent too much time or money gambling.
__ I thought too much about gambling.
__ I thought too much about sex.
__ I engaged in sexual behavior that felt out of control or went against my values.
__ I got involved in too many romantic or sexual relationships at once.
__ I overate and went on eating binges.
__ I forced myself to vomit after eating.
__ I spent too much mental energy or time on work.
__ I obsessed too much about _____.
__ I engaged in other compulsive behaviors, such as _____.

List any other relapse warning signs related to your specific psychiatric disorder(s) or addiction. For example, some people with bipolar disorder say they have trouble sleeping or start missing the high associated with mania.

_____
_____
_____

Go back and review the list of warning signs. Choose two that you have experienced in the past or that could occur in the future. List these warning signs and three steps you can take to manage each.

Relapse warning sign #1:

Coping strategies that I can use to manage this warning sign:

Relapse warning sign #2:

Coping strategies that I can use to manage this warning sign:

_____

_____

_____

Lisa's Warning Signs and Coping Strategies

"A big warning sign for me, for both of my disorders, is starting to believe that I can smoke pot and be okay if I just stay away from the hard stuff, like crack cocaine. To cope with this thought, I take the following steps: (1) I remind myself that pot always leads me back to cocaine. (2) I remind myself that when I smoke pot, I stop taking medication for my schizophrenia and usually end up in the hospital again. (3) I tell my sponsor right away when I feel like smoking pot. (4) I go to a dual recovery meeting to talk about my desire to get high, and I listen when others talk about what they did to cope. (5) I tell myself that I *can* do it, that I *can* resist any desire to get high on pot. I know that if I do these things, I won't relapse."

FIVE

DAILY SYMPTOM AND PROBLEM CHECKLIST

If you pay close attention to your thoughts, feelings, behaviors, mental health symptoms, and desires to use alcohol or other drugs to get high, you will be able to spot relapse warning signs early. This will make it easier to take action. Keeping a daily checklist can help you keep on top of your recovery and reduce your relapse risk.

On the chart on pages 22–23, rate the severity of the symptoms or problems listed in the chart. Put your rating next to the symptom or problem each day of the week, using the scale of 0 to 10.

When tracking your daily symptoms or problems, look for increases in your ratings over a period of time. An increase could mean that you are getting sicker or that you are close to an alcohol or other drug relapse. For example, Betty's usual rating for her symptoms of anxiety and depression was three or four. Recently, both these ratings jumped to six. This told her that her symptoms were getting worse. She alerted her therapist, and they worked together on ways to reduce her feelings of anxiety and depression.

> When tracking your daily symptoms or problems, look for increases in your ratings over a period of time.

Mike's usual rating for suicidal thoughts was one or two. This rating recently shot up to seven. But he followed his plan to let his doctor know about his increased ratings. They worked together, and Mike was able to get over his thoughts of hurting himself without going back to the hospital.

Bill had rated his obsessions and cravings for drugs at three or lower for several months. Recently, however, his rating rose to eight. He immediately talked this over with his sponsor and members of his NA group, who helped him figure out what triggered his drug cravings. As a result, Bill successfully resisted giving in to his cravings and getting high.

The sooner you catch changes in your symptoms or problems, the quicker you can take action. If some of your symptoms are more or less always present, a relapse would mean that a symptom worsened considerably. For example, Sandra still hears voices (hallucinations) even though she takes her medication and sees a therapist. She has learned to live with the voices, but she lets her doctor and therapist know if the voices get much stronger and interfere with day-to-day living.

Recovery Activity

Daily Rating of Symptom or Problem Severity

0	3	5	7	10
None at all	Mild	Moderate	Strong	Extreme

SYMPTOM OR PROBLEM	M	T	W	Th	F	S	S
obsessions/desire to use substances							
socializing with negative people							
pressures from others to use substances							
low motivation to change or work my plan							
not enough fun in my life							
not enough structure or direction in my life							
difficulty managing my feelings							
anger							
anxiety							
boredom							
depression							

Duplicating this page is illegal. Do not copy this material without written permission from the publisher.

SYMPTOM OR PROBLEM	M	T	W	Th	F	S	S
emptiness							
loneliness							
violent thoughts or behaviors							
self-harm, or suicidal thoughts or behaviors							
problems with sleep							
problems with appetite							
confused, disorganized, or racing thoughts							
false beliefs (delusions)							
hearing voices (hallucinations)							
impulsive actions (acting before thinking)							
avoiding others and isolating							
lying to or conning other people							
other symptom or problem (write in):							
other symptom or problem (write in):							
other symptom or problem (write in):							

Duplicating this page is illegal. Do not copy this material without written permission from the publisher.

SIX

MANAGING FEELINGS TO REDUCE RELAPSE RISK

Learning to identify and manage feelings, both positive and negative, are important parts of recovery from co-occurring disorders. Coping with feelings can improve your mental health and your relationships with other people. At the same time, it can lessen the chance of using alcohol or other drugs again.

Some of the more common feelings associated with relapse include anger, resentment, anxiety, worry, boredom, emptiness, euphoria (feeling really high), fear, panic, guilt, loneliness, and shame. You can expect to experience many different feelings during recovery. It is not whether you experience a feeling but how you cope with it that matters. For example, everyone gets angry at times. But while some people express it appropriately, others let it build up inside. This can contribute to depression. Other people "let it all hang out." They say or do whatever they want when they are angry, without thinking about others. This can damage relationships or contribute to guilt.

> You can expect to experience many different feelings during recovery.

While much attention is given to understanding and accepting uncomfortable feelings such as boredom, anxiety, or depression, it is just as important to be able to express positive feelings, such as love and caring. This enriches your life, makes you feel better, and strengthens your relationships with others.

The recovery activity that follows will help you identify the feelings you want to work on and develop a plan to do so. Some steps are then suggested to help you cope with feelings. Finally, you can read what two other people in recovery do to cope with specific feelings.

Recovery Activity

Choose two feelings that you want to work on. Then list steps you can take to cope with each of these feelings.

Feeling #1:

_____

Coping strategies that I can use to manage this feeling:

_____
_____
_____
_____
_____
_____

Feeling #2:

_____

Coping strategies that I can use to manage this feeling:

_____
_____
_____

_____

_____

_____

These steps can help you cope with the feelings you experience.

- *Recognize your feelings and give them names.* Admit your feelings. Be aware of how they show in your body language, thoughts, and behaviors. For example, some people get edgy and pace when anxious or angry. Others cry a lot or feel slowed down when they feel very depressed.

- *Try to figure out the cause(s) of your feelings.* Whether you feel anxious, depressed, or lonely, try to figure out why you are feeling this way. Then you can work on how to deal with the problem. For example, if you feel lonely and figure out that this is caused by problems communicating with others, then you know you have to improve your skills in this area. This may help you get close to others and feel less lonely.

- *Evaluate the effects of your feelings and how you cope with them.* If you openly express your feelings all the time or if you keep them inside, what usually happens? For example, if you hold anger inside all of the time, you may get headaches or feel depressed. Or you may hold grudges and avoid other people. If you always focus on expressing sadness and depression, you may push others away. They may get tired of hearing over and over about your upset feelings.

- *Identify ways to deal with your feelings.* A *verbal* strategy is to share your feelings with others. A *thinking* strategy is to talk yourself out of feeling a certain way. An *action* strategy is to get involved in physical activity to take your mind off your feelings or to release tension. For instance, if you feel bored and miss the excitement of getting high, you can tell yourself, *I'm not going to let my boredom*

Duplicating this page is illegal. Do not copy this material without written permission from the publisher.

drag me down, or *Sure, I miss partying, but it caused me more trouble than it's worth.* You can also get involved in fun activities to keep you busy and reduce your boredom.

- *Rehearse or practice new ways of coping.* Some people find it helpful to first practice expressing their feelings before they actually share their feelings with others. Perhaps you want to tell the important people in your life that you love or care about them. Or maybe you want to tell a family member that you feel upset and hurt about something he or she said to you. If you practice ahead of time, you will be more comfortable expressing your true feelings in the actual situation. It is kind of like practicing your speech out loud before presenting it in front of a group of people.

- *Put your new strategies into action.* As with any other skill, you have to use your strategies if they are to help you. Start with the easier situations first. For example, if you are working at expressing feelings toward people who have upset you, try it first with people who are likely to understand you and accept your feelings.

- *Evaluate the results of using new coping strategies.* Looking at the results of trying new coping strategies helps you fine-tune ones that work and get rid of those that do not.

April's Plan to Deal with Loving Feelings

"My addiction, self-centeredness, violence, and self-destructive behavior ruined many of my relationships. As a result, I became lonely and depressed. Now that I've been clean for a while, I feel ready to do more work on showing kindness and love to others. The first thing I have to do is not say hurtful things or hurt other people physically, because this messes up any progress I make. My therapist and I have discussed some things I can do to improve how I show love to others. It has to show more in what I do than in what I say.

"I'm doing many things to improve how I deal with loving feelings: (1) I call my parents every week, just to talk with them. I don't use these talks to ask for anything or get nasty to them like I used to but just to let them know I'm thinking about them. (2) I say something nice to another person at least once a day. (3) I send cards and gifts to my nephews for their birthdays and other special occasions. (4) I volunteer four hours a week at a rehabilitation center to help people with physical disabilities. (5) I'm working at breaking my self-defeating pattern with men. I usually tried to sabotage the relationship when I started feeling close, but I'm learning to cope with my fears so I don't run away when things are going well."

Al's Strategies to Cope with Anger

"I used to hold all my anger inside. It would build up and make me feel miserable and depressed. Then I'd get drunk and let it all hang out. The problem was, I'd do and say things that hurt other people. Now I do things differently. Sometimes I talk right to the person I'm mad at. If I have trouble doing this, I talk about my anger with my therapist or sponsor. This always helps me sort things out. To break the pattern of holding anger inside, I take a few minutes each night to do an 'anger check.' I review the day to see if I'm still holding on to any resentments or angry feelings. That way, I catch anger early and then figure out what I can do.

"I've had a lot of deep-seated anger inside me from things that happened while I was growing up. Talking things out in therapy and trying to forgive others for what they did to me were necessary for me to let go. Believe me, it wasn't easy to do. I still sometimes have trouble dealing with anger at certain people. But things are sure a lot better now. Getting angry is no longer a big excuse to get drunk."

SEVEN

COPING WITH NEGATIVE THOUGHTS TO REDUCE RELAPSE RISK

The way you think about yourself, your future, your illnesses, and your recovery affects how you feel and act. If your thinking is negative, you may more easily relapse to alcohol or other drug use or to your psychiatric illness. Learning to identify and change your negative thinking is another useful tool to prevent relapse.

Recovery Activity

The following are examples of negative thinking. Place a check next to the items that you believe apply to your usual way of thinking.

__ I make things out to be worse than they really are.
__ I think in terms of black and white and have trouble seeing things in degrees.
__ I usually expect the worst possible thing to happen to me.
__ I tend to have many more negative thoughts than positive thoughts.
__ I usually focus on the negative side of a situation.
__ I have trouble seeing the positive side of things.
__ I often think I'm not capable of getting better or changing my life.
__ I often think I'm not capable of staying off alcohol or other drugs.

___ I keep my bothersome thoughts to myself and don't share them with others.

___ I often think I need to be involved in recovery or treatment for only a short time.

___ I dwell too much on my shortcomings, problems, or mistakes.

___ I worry too much about the future.

___ I often think that life isn't worth living.

___ I often think a few drinks, joints, pills, lines, or hits off the pipe can't hurt me.

___ I think I'll hurt someone if I don't learn to control my angry or violent thoughts.

Choose two statements that you checked and write them in the following spaces. Then, for each thought, list two new thoughts that can replace the negative one. (For example, "I often think I need to be involved in recovery for only a short time" can be replaced by "Even though I want to stop recovery, I know it helps me to stick with it" or "By being patient and continuing my recovery, I increase the chances of not using chemicals and coping with my depression.")

Negative thought #1:

_____

New thoughts to challenge or replace this negative thought:

_____
_____
_____
_____
_____
_____

Duplicating this page is illegal. Do not copy this material without written permission from the publisher.

Negative thought #2:

_____

New thoughts to challenge or replace this negative thought:

_____
_____
_____
_____
_____
_____

Changing negative thoughts or beliefs takes time and practice, just like all of the other recovery tasks. Here are some suggested strategies that may help you change your negative thinking.

- *Be aware of your negative thoughts.* Try to catch yourself when you are thinking negatively. If you become aware of your negative thinking, you will be in a position to challenge and change it.

- *Challenge your negative thinking.* When you are having negative thoughts, challenge them. For example, if you have a job interview coming up and think, *I'm going to do poorly*, ask yourself what evidence you have that you will do poorly. Then tell yourself, *If I prepare for the job interview, I'll feel more confident.* Or suppose you are going to visit your parents and think, *I'm going to have a rotten time.* Challenge this by saying, *It doesn't always go well when I visit Mom and Dad, but I'm going to make the best of it. Besides, even though they complain, I know deep down they want to see me.*

- *Focus less on the negative and more on the positive side of a situation.* Instead of always seeing the glass as half-empty, look at the other side. Remind yourself of the positive. Suppose your AA or NA sponsor or a family member said that you were setting yourself up to relapse. Instead of having negative thoughts about that person and about yourself, you might think, *It's hard to hear the truth, but maybe he or she was right. Just because this person criticized me doesn't mean I'm not capable of doing okay or that I'm a bad person. It also doesn't mean that he or she is a jerk because of saying something that was hard for me to hear.*

- *Take a look at your progress and accomplishments from time to time.* Sometimes you can counter negative thoughts about yourself or your recovery by reviewing your progress and accomplishments. When you are having a rough time, this can help you see the bigger picture. Even if things do not always go well, that does not mean you do not deserve to compliment yourself for the efforts you put forth in recovery.

- *Remind yourself of the benefits of recovery.* Recovery offers many benefits, even if it may not seem like it at a given time. If you remind yourself of the actual or potential benefits of recovery, you can help yourself when you think things are going too slow or things are not going well. This can help you see the big picture and the long-term benefits of recovery from co-occurring disorders.

- *Make positive statements to others.* One way to decrease negative thinking and increase positive thinking is to say positive things to others. For example, let's say your daughter came home with a report card that was not as good overall as you had hoped. Rather than criticize her, you might compliment her for the good grades she did get and tell her you want to help her work at bringing up some of her other grades. Or suppose a friend or a co-worker does something nice for you; you can tell that person you appreciate what he or she did.

- *Keep a journal.* Write down positive thoughts or positive things that happen to you. Try to write at least a couple of positive statements each day, no matter how small they may seem.

- *Recite slogans or the Serenity Prayer.* These tools of recovery can help you accept the things you cannot change and change your thoughts to more positive ones. Slogans such as "This, too, will pass," "Think before you drink," and "One day at a time" can help you get through rough times.

EIGHT

DEVELOPING AND USING A RELAPSE PREVENTION SUPPORT SYSTEM

No one can recover alone. It is important to develop and use a support system as part of your recovery. You need a network of people who can support your recovery, people you can lean on during rough times.

Your support system usually includes the professionals who provide your treatment, such as your doctor, therapist, or case manager; AA, NA, CA, or DRA support group sponsors or members; close friends; and family members. These should be people with whom you have regular contact and with whom you can share your thoughts, feelings, and struggles. Ideally, people in your network should be honest with you and tell you if you are slacking off your recovery program or acting in ways that increase the chances of relapse. People in your recovery network should be willing to help you if you relapse to your psychiatric illness or your addiction.

> You need a network of people who can support your recovery, people you can lean on during rough times.

You can use your recovery network in many ways: to let others know what you are working on in your recovery, for emotional support, to discuss a problem, to discuss thoughts about dropping out of treatment, to talk through strong desires to use alcohol or other drugs, or to find companions for social or recreational activities. Talking regularly with members of your network, such as your sponsor or counselor, can help you identify problems early and make plans to deal with them before a relapse occurs.

Sometimes other people notice relapse warning signs before you do. You may find it helpful to ask members of your support network to point out any warning signs that they notice. Keep in mind, however, that it is your responsibility to take steps to cope with these warning signs if someone points them out.

Individuals who have a solid support system are more likely than others to maintain their recovery. They are more likely to feel secure because they have a network of people they can rely on to support their recovery efforts and help with problems.

Recovery Activity

List the names and phone numbers of five people you can rely on for support and help in recovering from co-occurring disorders.

Person #1 and phone number:

_____

Person #2 and phone number:

_____

Person #3 and phone number:

_____

Person #4 and phone number:

_____

Person #5 and phone number:

_____

Do you have a sponsor in AA, NA, CA, or DRA? ___ Yes ___ No

If no, how could a sponsor help you and what prevents you from getting a sponsor?

_____
_____
_____
_____
_____
_____

List some benefits of a relapse prevention support network. (Example: "I'll have people who understand my problems and who can support me during rough times. But I'll also have positive people I can spend time with and have fun with without worrying about alcohol or other drugs.")

_____
_____
_____
_____
_____
_____

List some ways that members of your support network can help you. (Example: "My wife can help me by telling me straight out if she thinks I'm slipping in my program. My sponsor can help me by guiding me through the Twelve Step program.")

_____
_____
_____
_____
_____
_____

NINE

COPING WITH EMERGENCIES

No matter how hard you work at recovery, there is always a chance that you could relapse to your psychiatric illness or your addiction. No one is immune from relapse.

It is good to prepare for emergencies ahead of time. This way, should you relapse, you can catch it early and take action to get back on track quickly. Some people experience psychiatric symptoms or use chemicals for many months before they decide to take action and get help.

If your psychiatric symptoms return or worsen, or if you start using alcohol or other drugs, seek help right away. If you become severely depressed, severely agitated, suicidal, homicidal, psychotic, or unable to take care of your basic needs for food, shelter, or safety, contact your doctor or the nearest emergency room; you may need to be in a psychiatric hospital. If you resume using alcohol or other drugs and get physically hooked again, you will need to enter a detoxification clinic.

> If your psychiatric symptoms return or worsen, or if you start using alcohol or other drugs, seek help right away.

Because some psychiatric conditions cause the affected person to deny the problem or refuse help, involuntary hospitalization may be needed for safety's sake. If your psychiatric illness(es) is of a nature (schizophrenia and other psychotic conditions) or severe enough that psychiatric hospitalization is a possibility, be sure to talk about this with members of your support network so that they can do what is best for you in an emergency.

Likewise, you might deny that using chemicals again is a problem, or you might refuse attempts from someone to help you following a severe relapse to your addiction.

Preparing for possible emergencies ahead of time with your support network can aid you in getting the help you need if things get bad. Let the people in your support network know how you want them to help. Put your plan in writing as a reminder, because if you get sick again, you might deny that you ever had such a discussion with your support network.

Other types of emergencies are not as drastic, but you should prepare for them nonetheless. For example, think about what steps to take should you go back to drinking or using other drugs, before you get physically or mentally hooked again. If you start thinking about hurting yourself again, you need an action plan to follow before your thinking gets worse and you actually hurt yourself.

Recovery Activity

Steps I can take if I return to alcohol or other drug use:

_____
_____
_____
_____
_____

Steps I can take if I have a psychiatric emergency:

_____
_____
_____
_____
_____

My family or members of my support network can help me in an emergency by taking these steps:

_____
_____
_____
_____
_____
_____

I would need to go into the hospital for help if I experienced any of the following symptoms or behaviors:

_____
_____
_____
_____
_____
_____

Keep important information where you or others can quickly find it should you relapse and need help. This information should include the names and phone numbers of your doctor and therapist, the phone number of your insurance company and your policy number, your psychiatric diagnoses, a list of medications, and dosages of each medication.

Make sure you talk about your emergency plan with your family, your treatment team, and other members of your support network. Remember: They are there to help you and support you. The best way to head off emergencies quickly is to ask for help immediately. Once things settle down, you can try to figure out what may have caused the emergency.

TEN

SUMMARY OF STRATEGIES FOR RECOVERY AND RELAPSE PREVENTION

Recovery is an ongoing process. It demands that you work hard to make changes in yourself and your lifestyle. Staying off alcohol and other drugs and reducing your mental illness symptoms require you to do your share of the work. You have to take responsibility for following your recovery and relapse prevention plan.

The following are actions you can take to help yourself in recovery from your psychiatric illness and your addiction. Taking these steps will also lessen the chances of relapse.

> Staying off alcohol and other drugs and reducing your mental illness symptoms require you to do your share of the work.

- *Keep all of your treatment sessions with your doctor or counselor.* Poor treatment adherence is one of the major causes of relapse to chemical dependency and psychiatric illness. If you have a valid reason for missing a session or being late, call your doctor or counselor to explain why you cannot make the session or why you will be late. Do not fool yourself or others by creating poor excuses for missing appointments.

- *Take your medication only as prescribed by your doctor and renew your prescriptions on time.* Do not take too much or too little medication or take other people's medication. Make sure you renew your prescriptions on time so that you do not go without medicine for even a single day. If you have questions or are bothered by side effects of medicine, talk to your doctor, counselor, or pharmacist right away.

- *Know your relapse risk factors and early warning signs.* Relapse risk factors are the situations or experiences that make you vulnerable to using alcohol or other drugs. They are also situations or experiences that affect your psychiatric illness. Warning signs may be general or more specific to your particular disorders. Knowledge of risk factors and warning signs can be used to plan strategies to manage these.

- *Participate in support groups.* Attend AA, NA, CA, or other addiction support group meetings. Attend DRA or mental health support group meetings. Meetings offer education, support, encouragement, and guidance. They give you the chance to relate to others with similar problems and learn from them.

- *Get and use a sponsor.* If you have a sponsor, talk with him or her every day. If you do not have a sponsor, set a specific date by which you will get one. A sponsor can help you work the Steps, attend meetings with you, or talk with you about recovery and relapse issues. A sponsor can teach you the ropes and mentor you as you get involved in the program.

- *Work the Twelve Step program of AA, NA, CA, or DRA.* The Twelve Steps provide a framework to change yourself for the better, which in turn may lower your relapse risk.

- *Control your emotions.* Feelings or emotions are an important part of life. Be aware of your feelings and learn to manage and share both positive (love, caring) and upsetting (anger, anxiety) feelings with others. Also, be aware of the feelings of others so you can convey empathy and understanding to them.

- *Change negative thinking.* Catch yourself when your thinking is too negative. Work hard to reduce negative and increase positive thoughts. Challenge negative thoughts that drag you down. Practice saying positive things to others.

- *Talk with another person from your support system every day.* Daily contact with your support system can help you keep your priorities in order. It also gives you a mechanism to get help and support immediately when you need it. Others who know you well may be able to spot early warning signs, even before you are aware of them. Maintain relationships with positive people who care about you. If you have trouble asking others for help or support, ask a counselor or your sponsor to help you learn the skill of making requests from others.

- *Be open and honest with mental health and addiction professionals.* Talk with your counselor or doctor about changes in symptoms, upsetting feelings, thoughts and desires to use alcohol or other drugs, thoughts of hurting yourself or another person, or other things that bother you. Talk about your desires to stop taking medications, stop going to your treatment sessions, or stop attending support group meetings. Talking about problems and struggles may prevent these from leading to a relapse.

- *Control your environment and the people you relate to in your daily life.* Get rid of alcohol, other drugs, and drug paraphernalia in your home. Avoid drug dealers and other people who are getting high or partying. Avoid people whose negativity or hostility drag you down. Spend time with positive people who want to support you.

- *Rely on your spirituality.* Pray, read the Bible or other spiritual texts, attend services, or use your Higher Power to gain strength.

- *Create a positive lifestyle.* Do something fun or enjoyable at least once each day. Develop a schedule to add structure to your day. Get up, go to bed, and eat meals at regular times. Pay your bills on time and take care of your other responsibilities at home, work, and/or school. Address your problems head-on rather than avoiding or ignoring them.

- *Reflect on your life each day.* Finish a daily inventory to track how you are doing and to keep your eye on possible relapse warning signs. Remind yourself of the benefits and gifts of recovery. Acknowledge your progress and the work you have put into your recovery.

- *Read recovery literature on a regular basis.* The more you understand about your disorders, the more control you will feel over your life. Ask your doctor or therapist for specific recommendations.

- *Keep a written recovery journal or file of your completed recovery assignments.* You can refer back to these as needed for a "refresher."

Recovery Activity

Other actions I can take to reduce the chances of relapse:

_____
_____
_____
_____
_____

If I follow my relapse prevention plan, I am likely to experience these benefits:

_____
_____
_____
_____
_____

ELEVEN

FINAL THOUGHTS

Spending time and energy using this workbook is a sign of your commitment to recovery. You deserve a lot of credit for learning about relapse prevention and developing a recovery plan. If you use the ideas you came up with as you completed this workbook, you increase your chances of doing well in your recovery from mental health and addictive disorders. People like you who work hard and stay active in learning and changing are usually the ones who do better in the long run. Remember, even small steps toward improvement are a good sign. They mean that you are headed in the right direction. By continuing to improve yourself and your lifestyle, you will cope better. Keep up the good work!